LET'S EXPLORE GERMANY

(MOST FAMOUS ATTRACTIONS IN GERMANY)

SPEEDY PUBLISHING

Speedy Publishing LLC
40 E. Main St. #1156
Newark, DE 19711
www.speedypublishing.com

Copyright 2015

Germany is the seventh most visited country in the world. Germany is well known for its diverse tourist routes.

Neuschwanstein Castle is a nineteenth-century Romanesque Revival palace on a rugged hill above the village of Hohenschwangau near Füssen in southwest Bavaria, Germany.

Brandenburg Gate is an 18th-century neoclassical triumphal arch in Berlin, and one of the best-known landmarks of Germany. Design of the Brandenburg Gate consists of twelve Doric columns, six on each side.

Heidelberg is a city situated on the River Neckar in south-west Germany. Heidelberg is one Germany's most popular tourist destinations.

Cologne Cathedral is a Roman Catholic cathedral in Cologne, Germany. It is a renowned monument of German Catholicism and Gothic architecture and is a World Heritage Site.

Insel Mainau is a "flowering island" on beautiful Lake Constance, covers an area of 110 acres and attracts many visitors with its beautiful parks and gardens, luxuriant with semitropical and tropical vegetation

Rothenburg ob der Tauber is a town in the district of Ansbach of Mittelfranken, the Franconia region of Bavaria, Germany. It is part of the popular Romantic Road through southern Germany.

Königssee is a natural lake in the extreme southeast Berchtesgadener Land district of the German state of Bavaria. Also known as the King's Lake, this area near Stuttgart is a walker's paradise.

96820393R00020

Made in the USA
Lexington, KY
24 August 2018